CAROLE BAMFORD

DAYLESFORD LIVING
INSPIRED BY NATURE

PHOTOGRAPHY BY MARTIN MORRELL

VENDOME

NEW YORK · LONDON

CONTENTS

INSPIRED BY NATURE 12

FLORAL TABLES 39

SNOWDROP BRUNCH 40

TULIP LUNCH 66

COW PARSLEY LUNCH 94

WILDFLOWER PICNIC 126

SWEETPEA GARDEN PARTY 156

HARVEST SUPPER 186

CHRISTMAS DINNER 220

SELECTED RECIPES

CELERIAC, PARSNIP AND APPLE SOUP 53

STEM GINGER CHEESECAKE WITH POACHED RHUBARB 79

ASPARAGUS, SPINACH AND WILD GARLIC TART 107

CHICKEN SALAD WITH CHARRED COURGETTES 141

GRILLED PEACHES WITH LEMON MASCARPONE AND MINT 169

SEARED VENISON WITH PICKLED BLACKBERRIES 199

BRUSSELS SPROUT TOP SALAD 233

ACKNOWLEDGEMENTS 254

INSPIRED BY NATURE

I've been fascinated by buildings for as long as I can remember. As soon as I enter a room, I can't help but start to think about how I would position furniture, add colour, texture and lighting to enhance a space, or even reimagine its proportions or structure. It's an instinctive reaction; my curious nature wants to explore possibility and expression.

In writing this book I've spent a lot of time reflecting on how I engage with a space and what inspires the way I create. I've thought about purpose and function and practical elements like scale, why I choose certain cupboard heights or angle a rug. But what I've also recognised is that filling a space is not solely led by necessity, practicality or taste. How we fashion our homes is mostly about feelings. The choices we make are a quest to incite emotion, both in ourselves and in others. Of course, how we design is an expression of our personality and taste, but it is also a measure of how we want to feel – and how we want others to feel – on entering our spaces. Our decisions allow us to create moods: eliciting comfort, instilling calm, fostering ease, and, above all, inspiring joy.

I've also considered what home means to me. Most likely it's similar things to many people: security, happiness, solace, memory. Home is a sanctuary – a place to escape to; somewhere to recharge my batteries, feel nurtured, soothed and comforted. And the need to protect and preserve that sanctuary is very important to me. Home is a tapestry – fragments of life that are pieced together through the objects, photographs and furniture that fill it, which in turn serve as memories, each bound up with the story behind their discovery.

My home is also a place to entertain – to invite people to share a meal, celebrate an occasion at a party or simply to gather. And as you'll see from the table settings that appear throughout the book, laying a table and making it look beautiful, seasonal and special is paramount to me.

I've been fortunate to have lived in different houses throughout my adult life, which has given me the opportunity to imagine, plan and design the interiors for each. When my husband and I first married we were living in Staffordshire, in his family home, but as our babies became children we began to think about the needs of a growing family and we both felt a pull to move closer to London. We eventually settled on a house on the outskirts of a traditional limestone Cotswold village called Kingham, in the west of England.

The Cotswolds is an area of England that I consider to be one of the most beautiful places on earth. I've been lucky to have travelled to some of the most remote and breathtaking corners of the world, and yet for me there is still very little that can rival the sight of the dawn breaking over the rolling hills that envelop our house, pockets of sheep huddled on the slopes and a mist gently lifting to reveal the green splendour of the valley that surrounds us, the morning dew still clinging to the grass. The expansiveness of the land that makes up the Evenlode valley is a sight that can still stop me in my tracks, and watching the landscape's colours turn with the season remains as captivating as the day we moved here.

Daylesford is not just my home, it's the foundation of my working life. Across the main road from the drive that leads up to our house is the farm that has become not only my passion but my purpose. When we bought Daylesford House and took over the farmland, the first thing we did was to convert it for organic farming. After years of being harmed by synthetic chemicals and fertilisers, the soil and the land needed time to heal. We started to see varieties of wildflower, pollinators and birds appear in the fields, while the soil became dark and moist, alive with worms and teeming with insects again. From those bare and tired fields, Daylesford blossomed into a thriving farm – and now a business too. At the heart of the farm site is our market garden and heritage orchard, where we grow a vibrant collection of organic fruits and vegetables.

> The expansiveness of the land that makes up the Evenlode valley is a sight that can still stop me in my tracks.

In the warmer months the animals we rear are spread amongst the pasture in the fields: dairy cows and beef cattle (including our rare-breed herd of Single Gloucesters), sheep, hens, turkeys and, in a pen at the top of the market garden, a few rare-breed Tamworth pigs. It's a diverse, mixed farm where the things that we grow and produce are sold in our shops in the Cotswolds and in London, as well as through other similar ethically minded retailers. We have our own bakery, dairy, smokery and creamery on site in the Cotswolds, as well as production kitchens that turn our produce and waste products, such as the animal carcasses and vegetable scraps, into stocks, stews and fresh meals. We also have our farm shop, a café and restaurant with a Green Michelin star, a garden room where customers can stock up on everything they need to furnish and work their growing spaces, a cookery school, wine bar, wellness spa and an enormous barn where we host events.

When I think back to how we started and I look around now, the scale of it can sometimes feel overwhelming. It was never my intention that it would grow in the way it has, and yet I know that with growth has come the opportunity to make a difference through what we do. I founded Daylesford with the aim of being able to feed my family in a better way and to work our land to give back to nature rather than taking from it. Today we can go beyond that. Daylesford has become a farm with over 40 years' experience practising sustainable principles, and we can pass on and share that knowledge to help others do the same. Scale means having the capacity to reach a wider audience, inspiring others to shop, eat or live in more conscious ways that care for our planet and its people. This is what continues to excite me and fuels my passion to keep doing more.

Besides being pressed on why I began to farm organically, the question I'm most often asked about Daylesford is where the aesthetic came from – what inspired the now distinctive look and feel of the farm shop. When we opened in 2002, there was a tendency for farm shops to look a little jumbled, haphazard and rustic, but I felt that we could create something in one of our old barns that was different: something that echoed the simplicity and purity of the produce we would be selling, as well as reflected the landscape of our surroundings. When I start the design

process of working with a building, my objective is always to honour and respect its character and features – I'm drawn to the past and to the heritage and tradition that these represent, but I also want to bring something fresh and modern to design; I love the juxtaposition of old and new.

Wordsworth wrote, 'Let nature be your teacher', and that is a philosophy I have always abided by. Nature is my touchstone, my greatest source of inspiration. Its rhythms and cycles guide the way I live and eat, and its colours and textures inform how I create. From the materials I work with to restore a building to the way I lay my table for a meal, nature is the seed from which everything grows.

Today a significant outlet for my creative expression and work with buildings and spaces has become the restoration and refurbishment of the pub buildings and cottages that are such an important part of the fabric of life at Daylesford. In 2012 one of the village pubs in Kingham came up for sale and its previous owners tried to convince me to buy it. I didn't know anything about running a pub but the challenge piqued my interest, as did the chance to ensure the survival of a much-loved local institution that could live

> Wordsworth wrote, 'Let nature be your teacher', and that is a philosophy I have always abided by. Nature is my touchstone and my greatest source of inspiration.

on for the community. When we began work on the pub site we decided to expose the architectural elements to honour the craftsmanship of the original building, which dates from the eighteenth century. By stripping back the plaster, the original stone walls were laid bare. Beams and door frames were patched; oak boards were revealed, and wattle and daub panelling was restored and re-rendered. By respecting the building's heritage, we were also able to remodel many of the parts we needed from reclaimed and recycled materials. And this is something that is also extremely important to me: refurbishment needs to be sensitive, sympathetic to the existing edifice and, above all, leave the lightest imprint possible (I've written in more detail about how I restored our pubs on page 59.) There are, of course, references to nature in the materials chosen for the furniture and furnishing: hazel wood was used for the side tables and oak sourced from storm felled trees on the estate became lamps and stools, while locally sourced chestnut was used to craft bedposts. Even the names and the colour palettes of our bedrooms were inspired by animals found within a three-mile walk of the pub, including hedgehogs, squirrels, rabbits and owls. We used bay-coloured bridle leather and rust-coloured hemp and linen for the deer room, pairing it with both natural linen and white bed linen for a subtle reference to the room's namesake.

The Wild Rabbit opened in 2013 and with it we established the aesthetic for which Daylesford has become noted: warm, understated elegance, paired with the feeling of being nurtured. 'The Rabbit' as it is affectionately known, is now one of four pubs we have in the Cotswolds, alongside The Fox, The Three Horseshoes and The Bell. We have also restored a group of cottages on the farm, in Kingham and in Daylesford village, a tiny hamlet next to our house. Each of the pubs and cottages has its own identity and character, expressed through its colours and décor, as well as through the bones of the building. As you will see from the photographs and vignettes of their interiors in the pages that follow, there is a natural visual language that runs through everything I do, and each building and venue echoes my style and taste. Each table setting celebrates and reflects the love of nature I've described through my choice of favourite seasonal flowers – the panoply of roses on this summer garden setting celebrates the abundance from my garden we enjoyed this year, and sets the tone for the tables that are to follow.

I'm also deeply inspired by the work of others. My bookshelves buckle under the weight of the many works that allow me to dive into the world of architects, interior and landscape designers, gardeners, furniture makers, artists and so many other craftspeople who have generously shared their creative processes in print. I have a vast collection of books – from the beloved stories I grew up with through to the biographies, novels and volumes of poetry I've loved as an adult. Cookbooks are a particular favourite – and I know my Arabella Boxer cookbooks would be some of the first possessions I'd reach for to save in a fire.

At a time when we are so drawn to the fleeting immediacy of the digital landscape, the sensation of holding a book, feeling its physical weight in your hands and carefully turning each page, remains a unique, unparalleled experience. Books are timeless treasures. They are portals to other worlds; they allow us to transport ourselves back in time, relive the emotions, challenges and lives of others and, above all, they allow us to dream. It is my love of books – as well as the generosity of the authors who have come before me – that has inspired the writing of this one. I wanted to open up my spaces and invite others in, to share my love of design, craft and creation in a way that gives anybody who cannot visit us in the Cotswolds a window into our world.

I hope that these pages might stir something in you: encouraging you to seek out the perfect lampshade for your bedside table, to install the log burner you've always dreamed of enjoying, to dare to hang the wallpaper you thought might be too bold or simply to make a mealtime feel that little bit more special by taking the time to dress your table. Above all, I hope that you will find joy in escaping, exploring and connecting with the boundless realms of your own imagination.

FLORAL TABLES

SNOWDROP BRUNCH 40

TULIP LUNCH 66

COW PARSLEY LUNCH 94

WILDFLOWER PICNIC 126

SWEETPEA GARDEN PARTY 156

HARVEST SUPPER 186

CHRISTMAS DINNER 220

SNOWDROP BRUNCH

SNOWDROP BRUNCH

No matter what time of year it is, a walk through my garden is always my first port of call for inspiration when I begin planning a seasonal table. Nature is abundant with textures, colours, sounds and scents, which can be easily overlooked if you tread the same path each day or your mind is elsewhere. By being truly present, grounded and engaged in your surroundings, you start to notice the beauty and potential of the world around you, from the clouds and constellations right down to the lichen on the trees, the morning dew on the leaves and the little shoots, bulbs or mushrooms that might be popping up through the forest floor.

Taking inspiration from nature right there in the moment is the simplest way to live and eat in tune with the seasons and your local landscape. It stimulates creativity in the kitchen, encouraging you to think on your feet, attempt a new recipe, or adapt a family favourite to make good use of the produce at your fingertips. Fortuitously, fruits and vegetables that are picked and prepared at the peak of their respective seasons always taste at their very best, so it isn't difficult to create something delicious and full of natural flavour. Nothing compares to the taste of those first spears of asparagus that come through in April, simply steamed until tender and dipped in a little homemade hollandaise. Or the flavour of a freshly picked strawberry in June, enjoyed while still a little warm from the sun, bursting with such a delicate, fragrant sweetness that it needs no adornment.

I think that taking note of what is in season, and just how short these seasons can be, instils a new level of respect for nature's bounty. Some native herbs, berries and vegetables can only be picked or found in specialist delicatessens for a very small window of time, so we ought to savour and celebrate these flavours. We are lucky to be able to forage a variety of ingredients from the farm's hedgerows and forests throughout the year, from chanterelles, rosehips and sloes in autumn to nettles and pungent wild garlic in spring. Easily identifiable by their spearhead shape, lush wild garlic leaves carpet the floor of our woods in Oddington from March until early May. They make a great seasonal substitute for spinach in quiches, pies, dahls and gnocchi, but my favourite way to use them is in a fragrant wild garlic pesto, by simply blitzing the leaves together with pumpkin seeds, olive oil, a little garlic, salt and pepper.

As well as inspiring the menu, the colours and textures of the landscape always sit at the heart of the table on which a meal will be served. In the autumn, I often use rich red fallen leaves from my Virginia creeper as place settings, alongside naturally shed deer antlers, foraged branches of brambles and shiny brown horse chestnuts to create a cosy, candlelit table – the perfect setting to enjoy a warming venison casserole and bowl of apple crumble after a long walk.

In early spring, I want to invoke the sense of brightness, optimism and fresh growth that you can sense is beginning to emerge in nature, so I gently lift and pot snowdrops from the garden to bring indoors. Their bell-shaped white flowers work wonderfully with neutral linens and crockery, perhaps accented with a little green embroidery or a decorative platter to tie in with the plant's long stems. Once the season is over, the snowdrops are returned to the garden, where they are carefully replanted to their original depth, and we patiently wait for them to pop up again the following January.

Celeriac, parsnip and apple soup

Peel, core and chop the apples and put them into a bowl. Pour over the lemon juice.

Heat the butter in a large lidded saucepan over a low heat. Once melted, add the chopped celeriac and parsnips along with some salt and pepper. Put the lid back on the pan and cook over a medium heat for 10 minutes without letting the celeriac and parsnips colour. Stir it from time to time.

Add the apples and lemon juice, put the lid back on the pan and cook for a further 5 minutes.

Add the stock and cream and bring to the boil, then turn the heat down and simmer for about 10 minutes, or until the vegetables and apples are soft. Transfer to a blender (or use a stick blender) to blitz the soup until smooth. Taste and season as necessary before serving.

SERVES 6

300 g / 10 oz tart eating apples
juice of 2 lemons
50 g / 2 oz unsalted butter
250 g / 9 oz celeriac, peeled and chopped
250 g / 9 oz parsnip, peeled and chopped
1 litre / 1 ¾ pints or 4 ¼ cups good vegetable stock
150 ml / ⅔ cup double (heavy) cream
sea salt and black pepper

MENU SUGGESTION

STARTER
Celeriac, parsnip and apple soup

MAIN
Shin of beef stew with Bledington blue dumplings and steamed kalettes

PUDDING
Lemon panna cotta with orange and fennel seed shortbread

When we first moved to Daylesford, the estate came with a herd of dairy cows, which we decided we wanted to keep, gradually breeding them back to become livestock that reflected our organic values. We chose traditional British Friesians, a pedigree that had historically been valued for its rich, creamy milk - and today, those beautiful black and white cows continue to produce ours. Their milk is balanced and wonderful for cheese making.

Such flavoursome milk allowed me to believe that we could begin to create our own cheeses, and so we transformed the barn opposite the milking shed into a creamery and began the development process for our first cheddar. The thought of tasting one that was properly aged, organic and local was the impetus that kept us going, because making cheese is a lengthy process, and it was only much later that we were able to taste our first 12-month aged truckle.

I am still very proud of the fact that it was the first organic cheddar produced in Britain and has gone on to win many awards. Today we also make our own Brie, blue and soft cheeses. These include our prized Single Gloucester, which has PDO status, and we are only one of nine producers in the country that are allowed to make it.

Not many people know that cheese is a very seasonal product because the density and flavour of the milk changes according to what the cows are eating. Our richer summer milk produces cheddar with a better depth of flavour while the smooth winter milk is better for our Adlestrop cheese - an adaptation of Welsh Caerphilly that we created ourselves at the creamery. I find the variance amazing - yet another reminder of what we gain when we work with nature, rather than against it.

> Our pedigree Friesian, rare-breed Gloucester cattle and organic pastures are the secret to our award-winning cheeses.

TULIP LUNCH

TULIP LUNCH

Whatever the occasion, whether it's a simple supper for me and my husband, a casual dinner party for friends or a big celebration, I like to make an effort with the table setting. Mealtimes have always been important to me. They are an opportunity to bring my family or friends together, to spend time celebrating and enjoying our food and to acknowledge the work and care that have gone into creating it. It feels right to honour that work by serving and presenting food as delightfully as possible.

When I'm planning a gathering, I'll almost always start with where everyone will sit. I usually seat people at long tables rather than round ones. It's just something I've always done because somehow it feels more intimate to me. Inevitably, as people talk across the table and the group conversations start, the chatter and noise levels rise and you've created a lively atmosphere. Depending on the occasion, I will often make a seating plan so that I can mix people up and introduce guests with similar interests who might not otherwise meet each other. I'll keep name placements very simple, just small white cards with handwritten names.

My inspiration and ideas for the table setting itself come from different sources. I will always begin by looking to nature and the flowers that are growing in my garden, and from there I'll start to plan the colours and the theme for the table. I generally keep flowers to a single colour, alongside foliage and other greenery, such as pots of herbs, and then add accents of other colours through the glassware or the linens and tablecloth. My favourite tablecloth at the moment is one of our hand-blocked prints from India. I won't use anything too heavily scented for the flowers and I try to let them be an embellishment rather than a distraction, so I will keep vases or the old glasses I often use to display them at a low height, so that nothing will ever be tall enough to block anybody's sight.

I also really like to decorate a table using other nods to a theme or my surroundings. So, for an autumnal party, there might be vegetables, such as pumpkins and different sizes and varieties of squash, or for a table setting when we're on holiday, staying near the sea, I'll use lots of shells and pebbles. One of my greatest hobbies is collecting pebbles, shells and coral from the beach, and I love to display them. For Easter there might be silver or ceramic hens, and nests made from twine or willow foraged from our local hedgerows, alongside lots of bright yellow crocuses or primroses. Or, as I've done throughout this book, I'll theme a table around a single flower.

You can also be a bit more playful and do something unexpected when it's sunny. I remember a lunch party where I arranged for everyone to sit on hay bales, which kept things really light and informal. As the day rolled into evening, people stayed to watch the sunset, the music was turned up and there was dancing on the hay bales.

I've set trestle tables up on the beach, and had picnic parties on the sand, but the one place I really want to host a party is in a vineyard. I'd love to set up lots of long tables among the vines. The drama of the landscape would be such an incredible backdrop, and I think I could have a lot of fun creating a wine-themed tabletop with bunches of grapes, old wine bottles, crates and vintage coolers. It's something I dream about making happen one day.

Stem ginger cheesecake with poached rhubarb

Line a 20cm springform cake tin with greaseproof paper. Preheat the oven to 190°C/170°C fan.

To make the base, melt the butter in a small saucepan. Crush the biscuits – either in a food processor or by putting them in a freezer bag and bashing them with a rolling pin. Stir through the spices and stem ginger then mix in the melted butter.

Spoon the mixture into the base of the tin and press it down firmly and evenly using the back of a spoon. Put the base into the fridge to chill.

Place the rhubarb in a shallow baking tray. Mix the orange zest, orange juice and sugar together, then pour the liquid over the rhubarb. Place in the oven and bake for 30 minutes, or until just tender. Remove from the oven and allow to cool.

Strain the juice and transfer to a heavy-based pan. Heat over a medium–high heat and bubble to reduce until thick and syrupy, then remove and allow to cool. Once cool, pour the syrup back over the rhubarb and chill in a bowl until needed.

Put the cream cheese into the bowl of a stand mixer fitted with the flat beater or into a mixing bowl and use a whisk to beat and soften it. Add the icing sugar and beat again until fully incorporated. Add the cream, vanilla, and both types of ginger, and whisk until firm.

Gently spread the mixture over the chilled biscuit base and level it using the back of a spoon. Set in the fridge overnight.

To serve, use a warm clean knife to cut slices of the cheesecake. Arrange the poached rhubarb alongside it and spoon over a little of the juices. Decorate with mint leaves, if using.

SERVES 6

FOR THE BASE
60 g / 2 oz or ½ stick unsalted (sweet) butter
180 g / 6 ½ oz ginger snap biscuits
1 tsp mixed spice
½ tsp ground ginger
10 g / ½ oz stem ginger, finely chopped

FOR THE POACHED RHUBARB
500 g / 7 oz or 1 cup rhubarb, trimmed and cut into 6cm lengths (if the stalk is quite thick, cut it in half lengthways)
grated zest and juice of 3 oranges
150 g / 4 ½ oz or ¾ cup caster (superfine) sugar

FOR THE CHEESECAKE FILLING
300 g / 11 oz or 1 ⅓ cups cream cheese
50 g / 1 ½ oz or ½ cup icing (powdered) sugar
150ml or ¾ cup double (heavy) cream
½ tsp vanilla extract
1 tsp ground ginger
15 g / ¾ oz crystallised stem ginger
mint leaves, to decorate (optional)

MENU SUGGESTION

STARTER
Purple sprouting broccoli and Parmesan with soft herb and caper dressing

MAIN
Seared rump of lamb, braised peas, radishes and wild garlic with buttered Jersey Royals

PUDDING
Stem ginger cheesecake with poached rhubarb

Planning a menu is something I love about entertaining. I have a huge collection of cookbooks and I can spend hours leafing through them to work out what I'm going to serve. Arabella Boxer's books are a constant reference point; I learned so much about planning a menu from her, and the River Café books are still favourites because their ethos of cooking and eating simply and seasonally mirrors my own.

So much of entertaining is making sure that everyone feels relaxed and has a good time – it's about the atmosphere you create, and I am a big fan of using playlists to set a mood; music is an essential part of the ambience. And I think it's also just about enjoying the process. I love welcoming people, seeing them enjoy themselves and watching their faces as they take in the different elements – be it the table, the food or other little details that I have added. I have grandchildren, so making sure that children are taken care of and can enjoy an occasion as much as the grown-ups is an essential consideration when I plan an event. If it's a big party, I'll sometimes provide some entertainment, such as a puppet show, and add touches that I know the children will enjoy.

It is often easier to entertain in the spring and summer months, when you can be outside, bringing people together in a more informal way, and where the food and table arrangements can reflect that – though of course, you run greater risks with the weather. I'll usually have a back-up plan, such as keeping Indian tents and plenty of blankets on hand in case it rains and the temperature drops, though I'm sometimes guilty of taking chances. I once held a summer lunch party in the middle of a huge field, with a beautiful view and not a building in sight, when the forecast was for heavy rain. I didn't have a plan B and I still thank my lucky stars that the weather held.

> I love welcoming people, seeing them enjoy themselves and watching their faces as they take in the different elements – be it the table, the food or other little details that I have added.

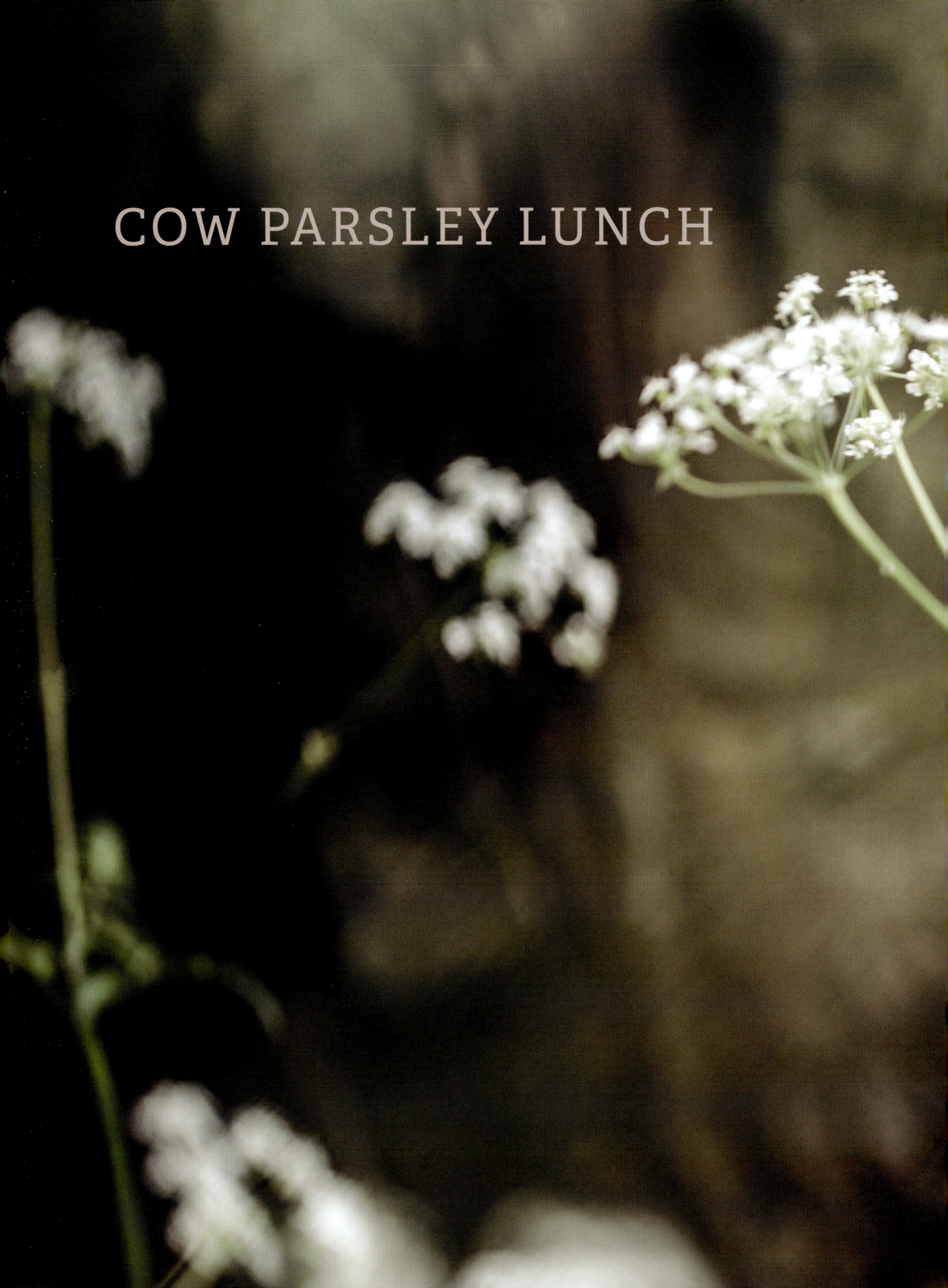

COW PARSLEY LUNCH

The complexity of textiles is something that has always captured my imagination. When I run my fingers along a handwoven piece of fabric, my eyes are drawn to the pattern of the weave, the thickness of the thread and the quality of the craftsmanship. Whether it is an eighteenth-century Genoese mezzaro from my collection of antique textiles or a rag rug made using scraps of cloth that may otherwise have gone to waste, handmade fabrics hold stories. They have a sense of history and spirit woven into their seams.

That story and past is one of the reasons I have such a fondness for upholstery. With a beautiful piece of fabric and the skilful hand of an experienced upholsterer, a tired, forgotten or outdated piece of furniture can be given a new lease of life, transformed into something truly unique and special that will be treasured for many years to come.

It is a love of fabrics and a reverence for exquisitely hand-crafted Indian textiles in particular that led me to establish Nila House, a centre of excellence in Jaipur. Nila works to support artisan communities across India and preserve the heritage and tradition of these crafts, which have been passed down through generations of families for decades – from cotton that is spun by hand and the irregular slub of handwoven khadi, to natural indigo dyeing, block-printing and embroidery. It is impossible not to marvel at the skill and patience required to master these traditional skills. With the march of fast fashion and advances in technology threatening to usurp their place in our world, Nila helps to preserve these ancient crafts and empower the artisans who work to sustain them. Each time I visit India, I can't help but return laden with intricate quilts, cushions and bedspreads. We collaborate with Nila to design bespoke prints and artisanal pieces for our Daylesford homeware collections, many of which you'll find dotted throughout these pages.

Textiles are an important part of dressing my tables. Aside from their practical use, napkins are one of the easiest ways to introduce colour, no matter what time of year it might be. I will often match them to the dominant flowers of the season: white for snowdrops, blue for cornflowers, pink for tulips and deep forest green for winter foliage.

Daylesford's 'Tiller' napkin and tablecloth collection has become one of the best-loved in our homeware range. They are made from 100 per cent washed linen by a small textile manufacturer in Portugal and you'll find them in many of the table dressings throughout the book, such as the dark indigo napkins in the table design in this chapter. I love their generous size and the fact that they have Global Organic Textile Standard certification, which means they have been produced to the highest standards of ecological and social responsibility, from biodegradable dyes and safe working conditions to the responsible handling of waste water and reduced energy and water usage.

When it comes to arranging napkins at the table, I take a very simple approach rather than anything too formal or fussy – perhaps a loose, unstudied knot or a simple rectangular fold to let the beauty and texture of the fabric speak for itself.

Asparagus, spinach and wild garlic tart

Preheat the oven to 160°C/140°C fan.

Grease a 20cm loose-bottomed tart tin. Dust a work surface with flour, roll out the pastry to 5mm thick, and wider than the tin. Lift the pastry into the tin, pushing it gently into the base and sides, then chill in the fridge for 30 minutes.

For the pesto, place the wild garlic in a bowl, add the pumpkin seeds, then cover with the olive oil and leave to stand for 5 minutes. Blend or use a pestle and mortar to pound the mixture until you have a consistency you like – chunky or smooth.

When ready to blind-bake, prick the base of the pastry case with a fork, then line with greaseproof paper – and fill it with baking beans. Put into the oven for about 30 minutes, until light golden brown, then remove the paper and baking beans, and brush the inside of the pastry case with the beaten egg to seal any holes. Bake in the oven for a further 5–10 minutes, until the base is golden brown. Remove from the oven and, when cool, carefully trim off the overhanging pastry with a small, sharp serrated knife. Reduce the oven temperature to 140°C/120°C fan.

Meanwhile, blanch the asparagus spears in salted boiling water for 3 minutes, then drain and plunge into cold water to stop them cooking.

Heat the olive oil in a saucepan with a lid, add the garlic and sweat until soft. Add the spinach, season with salt and pepper and cook at a medium–high heat for 1 minute, until wilted. Remove from the heat and squeeze any water out of the spinach, then transfer to a bowl. Stir through the Adlestrop, chopped herbs and season.

Fill the cooled pastry case with the spinach filling, then gently place the asparagus spears on top in a line. Put the quiche tin on to a baking tray.

SERVES 6

FOR THE PASTRY CRUST
plain flour, for dusting
1 x 250 g / 9 oz block of shortcrust pastry

FOR THE WILD GARLIC (RAMPS) PESTO
200 g / 7 oz or 2 ⅔ cups wild garlic (ramps), roughly chopped
90 g / 3 ¼ oz or ¾ cup pumpkin seeds
280 ml / 9 ½ fl oz or 1 cup olive oil

FOR THE FILLING
2 large eggs, plus 1 beaten egg for sealing the pastry
8 asparagus spears, tough woody ends removed
1 tsp drizzle of olive oil
1 garlic clove, finely chopped
300 g / 10 oz or 1⅓ cups fresh spinach
160 g / 6 oz or ¾ cup Adlestrop or Caerphilly cheese
1 heaped tbsp chopped chives
1 heaped tsp chopped tarragon
300 ml / 1 ¼ cups double (heavy) cream
sea salt and black pepper

Beat together the eggs, cream, salt and pepper with a fork, then pour the mixture into the pastry case to fill it. Drizzle a tablespoon of the wild garlic pesto over the top, put the baking tray with the quiche into the oven and bake for 45 minutes until it is both golden on top and set in the middle.

MENU SUGGESTION

STARTER
Dressed Cornish crab with herb salad

MAIN
Asparagus, spinach and wild garlic tart

PUDDING
Honey, lemon and thyme friands with poached apricots

I have a profound respect for the patience and passion that go into learning and then perfecting the skills required to craft something artisanal, and it's something I've always fought hard to share with other people, particularly by working with and supporting artisans.

Objects that are made by hand are, by their very nature, more sustainable than mass-produced or machine-made objects. Craftspeople need time to produce their creations; they work slowly, deliberately, with care, and in doing so they are naturally less wasteful, wanting to be mindful of the materials and resources they lean on.

It was when I first travelled to Japan that I realised that my love of the handmade could be defined. Unconsciously I had been embracing a philosophy, known as 'wabi-sabi', that runs very deeply through Japan's culture. Wabi-sabi is a concept that is hard to define precisely – there is no direct translation – but at its core is the need to celebrate the imperfect. Wabi-sabi supports the belief that there is a profound beauty in things that are incomplete, uneven or impermanent – that imperfections make things more meaningful.

I have always wanted to understand and learn more about wabi-sabi, so I turned to a book by Leonard Koren called *Wabi-Sabi for Artists, Designers, Poets & Philosophers*. Koren explains how much the wabi-sabi philosophy does in fact go beyond the aesthetic: it gently encourages us to lead a slower, more mindful way of life. It also reminds us that we are all passing beings on this planet and that our place here is secondary to nature's. Nature takes us through its cycles of growth, decay and loss, and although we are at its mercy, through wabi-sabi we can learn to surrender to and value both the joy and the melancholy found in each of these phases.

> Craftspeople need time to produce their creations; they work slowly, deliberately, with care, and in doing so, they are naturally less wasteful.

WILDFLOWER PICNIC

WILDFLOWER PICNIC

Of the five senses, smell is the most nostalgic. It can transport us straight to a moment in time, recalling feelings, places and memories. A scent can affect our moods by lifting our spirits, calming our anxieties and balancing our emotions. I imagine that you've caught the trace of a favourite or familiar fragrance unexpectedly and experienced its ability to make you smile or feel inexplicably happy. The scent of Bal à Versailles by Jean Desprez, which is the fragrance I wore on my wedding day, will immediately recall the joy I felt in that moment and can still shift my whole outlook and feelings in an instant.

Scent is something that has always been very meaningful to me. I love walking into a room to be met by a smell – fresh flowers, candles, a diffuser. Even if it's a scent I wouldn't choose myself, I can appreciate its presence: it will communicate the ambience its owner wanted to create in selecting it.

I use scent in lots of different ways at home. I love to bring the fragrance of nature indoors with big bunches of cut flowers and foliage from the garden in vases – or bulbs lifted and potted – and I also have candles burning at home from morning to night.

Scenting a room plays a role when I entertain: I'll either choose a bright, fresh fragrance with hints of citrus, or my favourite smells – geranium and lily of the valley – providing a vibrant backdrop to a party, filling the room with a delicious perfume. In the evening, if it's just my husband and me and we're trying to wind down, I'll choose something with a deeper pitch – more earthy and grounding, with notes of sage, sandalwood and nutmeg.

Many of the flowers I've used as the central focus of the table designs throughout this book were chosen for their fragrance, and the significance of the memories they evoke for me. Roses remind me of my daughter. On the warm days and weeks after she was born, I would push her around the garden in her pram, and the heady fragrance of roses in full bloom captures that particular year for me. Roses are the essence of English summertime and take centre stage on my tables throughout their season. For my winter tables, I use moss to accompany my snowdrops; its earthiness reminds me of the forest floor and of long family walks in the woods near our home in Staffordshire.

I grow a lot of sweet peas in my garden and again, their soft, subtle scent floating on the air is the smell of summer, so they feature frequently on my tables.

Some favourites had to be left out of this book because there wasn't room to include them all. Cow parsley, with its intricate structure and cloudlike heads that always make a dramatic statement on the table, takes the place of lily of the valley in May. I will always have pots of lily of the valley on my mantelpieces throughout the month – the flower signifies the joy of spring and the hope of the new season. I love its associations with the French May Day celebrations and the wonderful tradition they have of offering each other lily of the valley posies as a token of affection and to wish each other good fortune.

Nor could I include irises in this book, whose perfume I have always loved, and which now carry a very special meaning for me because my granddaughter is called Iris. These will always be the feature of a lunch table in spring – their pretty lilac heads with bright yellow stamens add such a cheerful pop of colour.

Built on a curve, our boundary wall separates the formal parts of the garden from the wildflower meadows which run down from our house to the farm shop. Not only does the wall act like a hedge, but it catches and retains the heat of the sun, and along it, we have various microclimates, one of which gives us the first strawberries of the season.

Just as the strawberries ripen, the meadows burst into life with a miscellany of poppies, ox-eye daisies, sweet scabious, chamomile, cornflowers and yellow rattle – it's the perfect time for a picnic in the sunshine. The beauty of setting a picnic table in a field of wildflowers is the simplicity of it. I love being as far away from the bustle of modern life as I can, so sitting in the middle of a field surrounded by nature, family and friends for a meal is my idea of heaven, and the sight and scent of the meadows in the early summer is breathtaking.

English wildflower meadows are a unique feature of our countryside but they are also an important part of traditional, organic agricultural practices, playing a vital role in the support of biodiversity. It saddens me deeply that modern, industrial farming methods mean that meadows have reduced by around 97 per cent across the UK since the 1930s and are now scarce. Their decline has had devastating effects on the biodiversity of our farms – and with fewer pollinators, the quantity of food we are able to grow will reduce too. But over 20 years of managing organic meadows on the farm has taught us a lot about how to help protect their flora and fauna and allow them to thrive.

Last year, we planted an additional 90 acres of dedicated wildflower meadows at Daylesford. These include lots of different kinds of flowers with a variety of pollen types that feed the bees and other pollinating insects – without whom our entire food system would collapse.

> English wildflower meadows are a unique feature of our countryside, but they are also an important part of traditional, organic agricultural practices.

Chicken salad with chargrilled courgettes and tarragon yoghurt dressing

To make the dressing, combine all of the ingredients in a small bowl and whisk to thoroughly combine. Chill until required.

To cook the eggs, bring a pan of water to the boil and carefully add the eggs. Simmer gently for 7 minutes and then cool under running water. Once cold enough to handle, carefully peel the eggs. Slice into quarters and keep to one side.

To cook the green beans, simply add to a pan of salted boiling water and simmer for 3–5 minutes until just tender. Drain, cool under running water and drain again.

Heat a chargrill pan until almost smoking. Slice the courgettes into 3 or 4 lengthways pieces and toss in the olive oil, salt and pepper. Grill on both sides, for 2–3 minutes until the courgettes are charred but still al dente. Remove to a plate.

To assemble the salad, tear the leaves from the little gem hearts and scatter them over a large platter. Arrange the green beans, courgettes and shredded chicken on top of the lettuce, followed by the quartered eggs. Drizzle the dressing all over the salad and finish with the chopped chives. Serve straight away.

SERVES 6

FOR THE TARRAGON YOGHURT DRESSING
100ml / 3 $\frac{1}{2}$ oz or $\frac{1}{3}$ cup natural yoghurt
100ml / 3 $\frac{1}{2}$ oz or $\frac{1}{3}$ cup mayonnaise
1 heaped tsp Dijon mustard
2 tbsp tarragon, finely chopped
1 tbsp chives, finely chopped
a squeeze of lemon juice
salt and pepper

FOR THE SALAD
4 organic eggs
200g / 7 oz or 2 cups fine green beans
200g / 7 oz or 2 cups courgettes thinly sliced lengthways
500g / 18 oz or 4 cups cooked chicken breast, shredded
1 tbsp olive oil
4 baby gem lettuce hearts
1 tbsp chives, chopped
sea salt and pepper

MENU SUGGESTION

STARTER
Heritage tomato panzanella

MAIN
Chicken salad with chargrilled courgettes and tarragon yoghurt dressing

PUDDING
Pink gooseberry and elderflower Bakewell tart

SWEETPEA GARDEN PARTY

SWEETPEA GARDEN PARTY

SWEETPEA GARDEN PARTY

I have always been curious about the heritage of old buildings, drawn to their sense of character, history and the intrigue of who might have lived or worked there before me. To discover a once-loved space that has since been left to ruin feels both disheartening and exciting. Storied buildings hold such potential, and as someone who is passionate about craftsmanship, I feel it is important to do what I can to preserve these sleeping beauties.

I would much rather breathe new life into an empty space, restoring the character already deep within its walls, than start a new building project completely from scratch. This is what we did with The Fox – a nineteenth-century coaching inn nestled in the village of Lower Oddington, which is about five miles from the farm – and where I arranged the sweetpea table for a summer evening garden party.

It was important to me that we restored The Fox sympathetically, in a way that considered our impact on the planet. We opted for local, natural and recycled materials wherever possible, using reclaimed timber for the construction, Cotswold stone for the masonry, and rolls of wool insulation made using the clip shorn from Daylesford's flock of Lleyn sheep to fill the walls.

This circular ethos is reflected in the interior design too. I am particularly proud of the leather banquettes, window seats and cushions in the bar, which were created using the hides from our organic beef cattle. We worked with a tannery in Bristol to transform this farming by-product into beautiful, supple leather using vegetable tanning and natural dyes.

This was then sent to a specialist leatherworker who crafted the furnishings for The Fox by hand. With enough skill and ingenuity, there really is no limit to the things you can create from homegrown materials that might otherwise go to waste.

Whether it's leatherwork, embroidery or pottery, there is something so special about handwork. When you look at a piece of art, sheet of wallpaper, a hand-painted lampshade or upholstered chair and know how much time, patience, skill and technique has gone into making it, it takes on a new level of meaning and importance. I believe these one-of-a-kind pieces have a different sort of presence. They add interest and character to a room in a way that something simply picked off a shelf does not. I wanted to add this feeling of warmth to the rooms above our pubs, so when we later began work on The Bell in Charlbury, I thought it would be a wonderful opportunity to draw attention to some of Britain's talented artisans.

At the Bell, we covered one of the 'Classic' bedrooms with a botanical 1830s-inspired sprig wallpaper that was designed and then block-printed by hand by artist James Randolph Rogers. James specialises in recreating historic wallpapers using hand carved blocks made from Northumbrian pear wood. It took James a month to carve the block for the sprig pattern, and a month more to print 150 sheets of wallpaper in a deep shade of indigo. As well as giving a truly distinctive finish, I love that the irregularity of the final markings makes palpable the energy and pressure exerted by the artist while executing his craft.

Grilled peaches with lemon mascarpone and mint

Place the whole peaches in a heavy-bottomed pan – big enough to accommodate them in a single layer. Add the sugar, then add the lemon juice and lemon zest and the vanilla extract. Cover with water and place a plate on top to submerge the peaches. Place over a low-medium heat and slowly bring to a simmer. Poach until the peaches are just tender, about 10–12 minutes, but keep checking them. Remove from the poaching liquor and leave to cool. Pass the poaching liquor through a fine sieve, then transfer it to a small pan and bubble to reduce the liquid to a syrup. Peel the peaches if you wish, then cut in half and remove the stone.

Gently fold the curd through the mascarpone (don't over-mix).

Lightly dust the peach halves with a little icing sugar, then put them on to the griddle for 1–2 minutes, until charred but not burned. Divide the mascarpone between serving plates and set either two or three peach halves on top. Drizzle with a little of the poaching syrup and decorate with fresh mint.

SERVES 4–6

6 whole peaches
100g / 4 oz or ½ cup caster sugar
juice of 2 lemons, plus the grated zest of 1 of the lemons
4 drops vanilla extract
100g / 4 oz or ½ cup mascarpone cheese
3 tsp lemon curd
icing sugar, to dust
1 mint sprig

MENU SUGGESTION

STARTER
Potted mackerel with cucumber relish and toast

MAIN
Grilled sirloin steak with harissa-roasted aubergine and butterbeans

PUDDING
Grilled peaches with lemon mascarpone and mint

Crewel work embroidery expert Sarah King is another artisan I had the pleasure of collaborating with on our furnishings for our pub in Charlbury, The Bell. Crewel work is a decorative embroidery that originated in the seventeenth century using crewel wool, which is a two-ply yarn made from long, fine fibres of wool. Traditionally, crewel work includes the use of vivid colours, intricate patterns and a variety of stitches, and its designs typically feature floral motifs, vines, animals and other patterns inspired by nature.

Anyone who knows me will also be familiar with my reverence for sourcing, collecting and – when it is needed – restoring antiques.

Many years ago at an auction, I bought a wooden four-poster bed that was hung with the most charming pelmet, seen here and overleaf, embroidered with lots of little nature-inspired motifs. Although still very beautiful, the fabric was quite timeworn in places, so needed restoring and extending slightly to meet the dimensions of a modern-sized double bed.

We think the original textile dates back as early as the seventeenth century, so Sarah had to work extremely carefully to refresh and replicate every individual squirrel, dog, flower and bird – each requiring a unique blend of English-dyed wool matched to the exact colours of the antique version. The final result was outstanding.

It is a rare privilege to experience the slow craft of an artisan like Sarah. In giving a new lease of life to this forgotten piece of furniture, she also helped to preserve the heritage of this specialised type of embroidery.

> Anyone who knows me will be familiar with my reverence for sourcing, collecting and – when it is needed – restoring antiques.

HARVEST SUPPER

HARVEST SUPPER

Harvest means gathering the food of the land, and it is of course a pivotal time on a farm – the culmination of months of work as we collect the fruits of the year's planting, sowing and tending to store as food for the winter. It is a moment of celebration but also of nervous anticipation. As the summer fades and the rusty, burnished tones of the autumn streak the fields and woodlands, we wait to see whether we will have a fruitful, abundant harvest, and if the year's hard work will yield the bounty of fruits and vegetables we need to provide for ourselves – and our customers – throughout the winter.

It's such an important marker in the year that we try to honour it annually through our harvest festival. Traditionally, these festivals were celebrated at the end of the growing season, which is usually in late September or early October. As soon as the last crop had been stored away, the community would hold a feast to celebrate this safe gathering-in. But since the start of the twentieth century, the tradition has evolved and there are many different customs and festivities around the UK. Celebrations hosted by churches and schools often involve food donations, which are then redistributed to members of the local community in need.

Ours is something I look forward to every year. It is a colourful and joyful occasion when the farm comes alive for a day of feasting and fun, with food stalls, games, music and plenty of opportunities to sample the best of the season's produce. It is a day to give thanks for the gifts nature's work has provided, and it also reminds us that if we don't look after and protect our planet, this bounty of produce and the beauty we find in the colours and many stages of the changing seasons will be lost.

Our celebrations follow more or less the same format every year. The Daylesford fire pits and barbecues are lit; there are lots of delicious offerings to taste from our bakery, patisserie, creamery and fermentary, and a bar serving Daylesford cider, craft beers and organic wines. We also showcase many artisanal foods and ingredients from our neighbouring producers. There's always a competition tent with prizes for 'most impressive cake decoration', 'largest harvest vegetable' and 'tastiest preserve'. We host an extremely popular and much-loved dog show, which includes categories such as 'waggiest tail' to 'dog most like its owner'. Our floristry teams put on lots of workshops and help participants of all ages make floral crowns. Children enjoy plenty of games and crafts, as well as opportunities to have their faces painted, meet some of our animals or watch sheepdogs herd our flock.

Seared venison with pickled blackberries, beetroot and creamed cabbage

Preheat the oven to 180°C.

Pickle the blackberries. In a pan, combine the sugar, red wine, red wine vinegar, water, star anise and rosemary. Bring to a simmer, stirring until the sugar has dissolved. Add the blackberries, set aside to cool and infuse for half an hour.

Next, place the beef stock or bone broth in a pan and bring to the boil. Simmer gently with the lid off until the liquid has reduced by at least a half, and is beginning to thicken a little. Whisk through the redcurrant jelly, season to taste and keep warm.

Season the beetroot generously with salt and pepper, wrap in foil and bake in the oven for around 30–40 minutes or until just tender. Set aside to cool slightly in the foil before unwrapping and removing the skin once cool enough to handle. Discard the skin and re-wrap in the foil to keep warm.

Blanch the carrot in boiling water until just tender. Fry the bacon in a pan until crispy, then cut into small pieces. Add the cabbage to the bacon with a splash of water. Simmer until the cabbage is just cooked but still retains its colour. Add the carrots, remove from the heat and set aside.

Set an ovenproof pan over a high heat and add the venison loin. Sear on all sides until golden before transferring to the oven to cook through for 12–15 minutes or until medium rare. Remove from the oven and set aside to rest.

Return the cabbage to the heat and add the double cream. Cook until the cream thickens and the vegetables have heated through, then check the seasoning before dividing between plates. Roll the venison in the crushed pink peppercorns and thyme leaves and slice. Arrange on top of the cabbage, dividing the beetroot between the plates.

SERVES 6

FOR THE PICKLED BLACKBERRIES
40g / 1 ½ oz or ½ cup caster sugar
40ml / ¼ cup red wine or port
40ml / ¼ cup red wine vinegar
40ml / ¼ cup water
4 star anise
2 rosemary sprigs
handful of freshly foraged blackberries

FOR THE VENISON
1 litre / 1 ¾ pint or 4 ¼ cups beef stock or bone broth
2 large or 4 small raw beetroot, washed, trimmed and halved lengthways
2 tsp redcurrant jelly
600g / 1 ¼ lb venison loin
4 tsp pink peppercorns, roughly crushed
stripped leaves from 4 thyme sprigs
sea salt and black pepper

FOR THE CREAMED CABBAGE
2 small carrots, finely diced
4 streaky bacon slices
½ Savoy cabbage, finely sliced
100ml / ⅓ cup double (heavy) cream

Pour over the warm jus. Strain the blackberries from their pickling liquid and arrange over the top of each plate before serving.

MENU SUGGESTION

STARTER
Roasted red kuri squash with balsamic-roasted red onions, pomegranate and rocket

MAIN
Seared venison with pickled blackberries, beetroot and creamed cabbage

PUDDING
Sticky marmalade puddings with vanilla custard

Deer parks have been a feature of English country estates since Anglo-Saxon times, when they were known as hays, after the hedges that surrounded them. Our home at Wootton in Staffordshire, where we began farming over 50 years ago, has over 1,500 acres of dedicated land for our 700 native red deer. They were the first, and are still the largest, privately managed herd in England.

Wootton deer park almost looks after itself. Yet as human activity has removed most animal predators and introduced many non-native tree species, we have had to take an active role in woodland management. This year an ash-tree blight has forced us to remove several diseased specimens that might infect others, giving us a glut of timber. We've recycled it for tables in our offices and lamp fittings for the cottages.

The herd expands or contracts depending on the demand for venison. We keep around 20 stags, 350 hinds, and the rest are the playful spikers and kids that bound through the fields at the slightest sound.

The cooler weather in early September heralds the start of the rutting season. The stags brandish their long, pointed antlers in competition with each other and, after mating, their antlers are cast. These are collected to be made into door handles, chandeliers and cutlery at Daylesford. Wootton gives us so much throughout the year and is a treasured part of our enterprise.

> We keep around 20 stags, 350 hinds, and the rest are the playful spikers and kids that bound through the fields at the slightest sound.

CHRISTMAS DINNER

CHRISTMAS DINNER

Christmastime is one of the great joys of the year for me. From making our Christmas pudding on Stir Up Sunday right through to New Year's Eve, it feels like there is a lightness in the air – a sense of anticipation and excitement at all there is to look forward to, organise and celebrate.

As someone who takes great pleasure in hosting, I often find the process of making the preparations as fulfilling as the day itself – and sometimes, even more so. This begins with decorating the house in early December. I prefer a traditional theme, with a palette of joyful reds, greens and glittering golds. We will always have a fragrant pine tree felled from the farm at the bottom of the staircase, lit up with lots of white fairy lights and all sorts of baubles that my family have collected over the years. Ever since my children were little, we have always displayed the same Nativity scene on a side table next to the tree. It's a charming reminder of how resonant the meaning of Christmas is for me, so it is wonderful to see my grandchildren play with those old wooden characters when they visit to peek at the presents under the tree.

Much of the foliage I use to decorate the mantelpiece and windowsills is foraged from the farm, making it a more sustainable way to bring colour, scent and a sense of all that is happening outdoors into my home. To create scale and a little drama, we wind heavy garlands around the pillars in the entrance hall. I think hanging a wreath on the door is a lovely, welcoming way to set a festive first impression for visitors, so ours are woven with generous bunches of greenery from the garden, including silver spruce, ivy, bay, white mistletoe, rosehips and, of course, holly with its scarlet berries.

Precious time with family and friends is one of the things most dear to me at Christmas, so I like to ensure the house is well provisioned for unexpected arrivals coming in from the cold. Being prepared means I can relax and simply enjoy their company. The pantry shelves will be laden with mince pies, seeded biscuits, preserves and fruit cake from the farm's bakery, and I will order a range of soft and hard cheeses from the creamery for everyone to pick away at.

A well-stocked drinks cabinet is always a good way to ease people into the festive spirit, so there will be a good supply of Daylesford's rosé frizzante and English sparkling wine chilling in the fridge throughout the month of December. For a quick and colourful festive cocktail, simply top up a small measure of homemade sloe gin with some cold sparkling wine to create a seasonal twist on the classic Kir royale.

On Christmas Day itself, I usually like to keep my table quite classic with white linens, crystal glassware and plenty of candles to create a cosy and dreamlike setting, though sometimes I'll bring in slightly more laidback elements, such as Daylesford's handblown Ledbury glassware, which has a more informal feel. With the table I've set here, I've chosen a very pared-back white and green theme, using white holly berries and hellebores alongside seasonal fruits, such as pears, but beautifully made paper crackers would be a good way to add colour and pattern alongside naturally vibrant holly berries, skimmia, pine cones and clementines. I like the idea of using handmade tree decorations as table gifts – a memento of a special lunch that can be taken home and admired for many more Christmases to come.

Brussels sprout top salad

Place the sprout tops, Brussels sprouts, parsley and fennel in a large bowl. Roughly chop the pumpkin and sunflower seeds and toss half with the ingredients in the bowl.

Whisk together all of the ingredients for the dressing in a jar and pour over the salad, tossing everything together again. Leave to sit for about 5 minutes to allow the sprout tops to soften a little before scattering over the remaining seeds and the blood orange segments.

SERVES 4

3–4 sprout top leaves, finely chopped
12 Brussels sprouts, finely chopped
4 tbsp finely chopped parsley
½ small fennel bulb, finely chopped
3 tbsp pumpkin seeds, toasted
1 tbsp sunflower seeds, toasted
1 blood orange, segmented

FOR THE DRESSING
3 tbsp lemon juice
2 tbsp olive oil
generous pinch of salt
lots of freshly cracked black pepper

MENU SUGGESTION

STARTER
Brussels sprout top salad

MAIN
Roast turkey with all the trimmings

PUDDING
Christmas pudding

Festive Daylesford cheeseboard

Throughout autumn and winter, preserving our produce becomes an important focus on the farm. Squashes, apples, beetroot, blackberries and pears are all transformed into chutneys and jams or carefully stored to ensure they last the winter. One of my favourite activities, partly because it has become so emblematic of what we do here at Daylesford, is the transformation of our apples into our Evenlode Orchard Cider.

Cider production remains an important and traditional part of Cotswold farming culture. In the 1950s, there were 15,000 acres of orchards in Gloucestershire, a figure that today has been reduced to only 3,000 acres. But thanks to Jez Taylor, who manages our market garden, we are reviving and continuing this tradition.

To make a good cider, you need a balance of sweet, acid and tannic flavours. Cider apples differ greatly from anything one would eat, but their sharp, bittersweet flavours are necessary for a complex, distinct juice. Jez uses a mix of Brown's, Sweet Coppin and Coat Jersey apples to make ours. All of these are old English varieties that we grow here on the farm. Jez and his team wait for the fruit to fall naturally in late October or early November. When the fruit falls on its own, it is perfectly ripe and that's when it will have the highest natural sugar content, which will give you the best flavour and alcohol percentage.

Jez and his team will press over 3,000 litres of juice in a single week, which will be naturally fermented and ready to bottle as cider a year later. The dry apple pulp from the presser is a brilliant component of our compost and feeds into the circular economy of the garden, allowing us to put nutrients back into the soil.

Cider production remains an important and traditional part of Cotswold farming culture.

ACKNOWLEDGEMENTS

This book reflects so much of the essence and spirit of Daylesford – seasonal growing and eating, timeless textiles, ceramics and furniture, buildings lovingly refurbished to offer warm and welcoming stays, the importance of being conscious and mindful consumers, the joy in life's simple pleasures, an easy picnic with friends or lunch as a family at home. In writing the book and watching it come to life, I've thought back on the early days – over 20 years ago now – and what's brought us to this point, and not a day has gone by in which I don't feel profoundly grateful for all that we've created and achieved.

None of Daylesford would be possible without the passion and commitment of my wonderful teams – I have a vision but they make the magic happen and I owe them huge thanks for all that they do.

Writing and creating a book is a very collaborative process and there are a few people that who have helped me bring the Daylesford world to life on these pages.

A very big thank you to Beatrice Vincenzini, my publisher and friend, for allowing me to create a book that I adore, for making it feel so 'me', and for your dedication and passion for the project. I've loved working with you.

And heartfelt thanks to the whole team at Vendôme Press, in particular Catharine Snow, for your attention to detail and steady hand, as well as Amy Tai and her team.

Martin Morrell, after so many years of working together you continue to capture my vision and my world with such a creative and considered eye and I will never cease to be amazed by your skill. Thank you.

Claudie Dubost, you brought my tabletops to life with elegance and grace and it is always such a joy working with you.

The beautiful flowers, foliage, fruit and vegetables on the tables were lovingly grown and foraged by Kim Robinson, Jez Taylor and Steven Gamble: you are all immense talents. Thank you to Gaven Fuller for the recipes, which embody the food Daylesford's customers enjoy every day.

Hugo Guinness, thank you for the wonderful illustrations that we have used for the book's endpapers.

And finally to Imogen Fortes and Catie Collins, for helping me bring this world to life on the page.

DAYLESFORD LIVING

First published in 2024 by The Vendome Press

Vendome is a registered trademark of The Vendome Press LLC

VENDOME PRESS US
PO Box 566
Palm Beach, FL 33480

www.vendomepress.com

VENDOME PRESS UK
Worlds End Studio
132–134 Lots Road
London, SW10 0RJ

Copyright © 2024 The Vendome Press LLC
Text Copyright © 2024 Carole Bamford
Photography Copyright © 2024 Martin Morrell

All rights reserved. No part of the contents of this book may be reproduced in whole or in part without prior written permission from the publisher.

Distributed in North America by Abrams Books
Distributed in the United Kingdom and Europe by Abrams & Chronicle Books

Every effort has been made to identify and contact all copyright holders and to obtain their permission for the use of any copyrighted material. The publisher apologizes for any errors or omissions and would be grateful if notified of any corrections that should be incorporated in future reprints or editions of this book.

ISBN 978-0-86565-432-7

Publishers: Beatrice Vincenzini, Mark Magowan, and Francesco Venturi
Editor: Catharine Snow
Contributing Editors: Imogen Fortes, Catriona Collins and Christopher Garis
Production Manager: Amanda Mackie
Designer: Roger Barnard
Endpaper Illustration: Hugo Guinness

Library of Congress Cataloging-in-Publication Data available upon request

Printed and bound in China by 1010 Printing International Limited